T0195741

THE
ART OF CARVING

THE
ART OF CARVING

EXCERPTED

FROM A WORK ENTITLED

The Honours of the Table (1788)

BY

THE REVD DR JOHN TRUSLER

Author of

The Principles of Politeness

&c.

"To do the honours of a table gracefully, is one of the out-lines of a well-bred man; and to carve well, little as it may seem, is useful twice every day, and the doing of which ill is not only troublesome to ourselves, but renders us disagreeable and ridiculous to others."

LORD CHESTERFIELD'S LETTERS

With a Biographical Note by S.M.
and an Appreciation by S.C.R.

CAMBRIDGE

AT THE UNIVERSITY PRESS

1932

CAMBRIDGE UNIVERSITY PRESS
Cambridge, New York, Melbourne, Madrid, Cape Town,
Singapore, São Paulo, Delhi, Mexico City

Cambridge University Press
The Edinburgh Building, Cambridge CB2 8RU, UK

Published in the United States of America by Cambridge University Press, New York

www.cambridge.org
Information on this title: www.cambridge.org/9781107619326

First published 1932
First paperback edition 2013

A catalogue record for this publication is available from the British Library

ISBN 978-1-107-61932-6 Paperback

JOHN TRUSLER
1735–1819

"In making me a clergyman, my father spoilt a good layman" wrote the author of *The Honours of the Table*—and a score more volumes, not counting a three-volume dissuasive from gallantry in the form of a novel. His innumerable sermons were for others to preach, for no Reverend Father in God shared his parents' longing to see the Doctor rewarded with good glebe and rectory.

He was, we may as well admit, a poor scholar; but his hundreds of syndicated sermons—sold to the cloth, at a shilling a time—enriched him above most of the incumbents who were thus enabled to preach from a "manuscript" printed in type so closely resembling handwriting as to deceive even the acutest of the elect.

That no hint of scandal should mar the efficacy of the Doctor's up-to-date ministry of the printed word, he saw to it that "the same subjects go not into the same neighborhood." Nor did he lack encouragement from dignitaries of the Church. Notwithstanding, an obscure clerical contemporary denounced the scheme as a "scandalous species of quackery," a severe description indeed for what the author's prospectus referred to as "the finest body of Divinity extant." The blow, however, was softened, for the Revd Mr Rivers refrained from printing these harsh words until after the Doctor, on completing twenty-five years of service, terminated his sermonising. By this time he was busy with the "Literary Society" established in the Trusler dwelling house (first in Red Lion-street, Holborn, and later in Wardour-street, Soho) to publish the works of deserving authors, himself in particular, while guaranteeing them what the booksellers did not—the full possession of their copyrights. A printing-press was installed and it was with the imprint of The Literary Press that *The Honours of the Table* appeared.

It was to feed the press that Dr Trusler laboured to compile a pettifogging *Guide to London*, *A Dictionary of Rhymes* and other remunerative odds and ends. On a larger scale, and with greater ambition, he brought out *Hogarth Moralised*, and, serially with pictures, *The Habitable World Described*.

His acquaintance with George Cumberland brought him into touch with William Blake from whom the Revd Doctor sought illustrations to one of his productions. The commission drew, instead of plates, two explicit letters in which the artist endeavoured to explain his sorrow that the Revd Dr Trusler was, from his point of view, "fall'n out with the Spiritual World, Especially if I should have to answer for it." "I feel very sorry" Blake wrote "that your Ideas & Mine on Moral Painting differ so much as to have made you angry with my method of study. If I am wrong, I am wrong in good company. I had hoped your plan comprehended All Species of this Art, & Especially that you would not regret that Species which gives Existence to Every other, namely, Visions of Eternity." In the same letter, Blake reproved Trusler for possessing an "Eye perverted by Caricature Prints, which ought not to abound so much as they do."

Failing to secure the co-operation of Blake, Trusler employed the Bewicks. But illustrated books were not the Doctor's chief interest. He preferred to write and publish handy, inexpensive and saleable repositories of elementary knowledge. Of these, *The Principles of Politeness*, a bowdlerised Chesterfield, had such a large sale that it inspired the Doctor to compile the work from which we have reprinted the following pages.

The Honours, on first sight, seems a curious exercise to come out of Westminster and Emmanuel, or, indeed, from anyone brought up in what the Doctor would call "the line of a gentleman." Yet its author had more excellent credentials for undertaking this than any other of his pious labours, for he was assuredly no layman where the good things of the table were concerned. Trusler's father was a born cook and practised the art professionally at the Marylebone-gardens, of which he was proprietor from 1756 to 1763. He was supported by Miss Trusler, our author's sister, who specialised in rich seed-cakes, plum-cakes and, above all, almond seed-cakes, "using none but loaf sugar and the finest Epping-butter." After the family retired from Marylebone, Miss Trusler delighted the palate of the West-end by supplying her famous cakes from a shop in Boyle-street, Savile-row. Doubtless Dr Trusler himself owed his interest in domestic management and the affairs of the kitchen and some of his knowledge of the arts of cooking and carving to the family tradition. If the proof of the pudding is in the eating—a long life is the best demonstration of indulging according to wisdom and experience. Hence, Dr Trusler's eighty-five years of life must have endorsed his advice with the maximum of authority for the carvers and eaters of his time.

S. M.

AN APPRECIATION

The Reverend Doctor Trusler's observation that no more useful or acceptable present could be conferred upon the rising generation of the year 1788 than instruction in the *Art of Carving* is not lacking in relevance to the present state of household œconomy.

For among such "accomplishments of a gentleman" as are still somewhat fitfully pursued, there is none that suffers more, whether from utter neglect or from imperfect execution, than the art of elegant carving.

How often are one's proper pleasures of the table marred by the spectacle of a host "hacking for half an hour across a bone, greasing himself, and bespattering the company with the sauce"; or blindly scattering shapeless slabs from a good sirloin; or scraping exiguous slices from a respectable leg of mutton!

That many of the present generation of householders should seek an easy way of escape is only one degree less reprehensible; to employ at a side-table the vicarious services of a parlour-maid, however deft, is to shirk what should be an integral part of the conduct of the domestic board and to deprive the guests of one of the purest of human pleasures—watching an artist at his work.

It is to be hoped, then, that Dr Trusler's manual will receive the earnest attention which it deserves, particularly as his text is embellished by a series of cuts which are admirably adapted to the needs of the beginner. Two of these cuts are wisely devoted to the Shoulder of Mutton, than which there is no joint capable of providing a more pleasing variety of sensation—witness the contrast between the rich quarry of wedge-like slices revealed when the first cut is made on the upper side and the smooth plateau of lean meat discovered when the joint is turned.

We could wish that Dr Trusler's pictorial representation of "a Piece of a Sir-loin of Beef," a joint with which every practitioner should be familiar, were a little more explicit. The position of the undercut ("the fleshy part underneath, which is by far the most tender") might with advantage be more clearly shewn, since the ladies of the company will certainly prefer a few toothsome slices from this portion of the joint; gentlemen, on the other hand, may prefer a larger and redder slice from the upper side.

Dr Trusler demonstrates the carver's anatomy

of many table-birds in commendable detail, but curiously omits reference to the Duck, a very popular dish for small parties and fraught with special danger for the ignorant carver. Let the beginner remember always that the attack should be begun upon the breast. If the bird be a well-fed one, this will provide a number of elegant portions for the ladies; after which the legs may be approached, due care being taken in the jointing.

But it would be graceless, indeed, to emphasise unduly such slight deficiencies as may be found in Dr Trusler's work. Rather let us record our thanks for his rightful insistence upon the elegancies of the table; let us, further, most fittingly honour his memory by a resolution to recover the lost *Art of Carving*.

S. C. R.

THE
HONOURS OF
THE TABLE

Rules for behaviour at table

Of all the graceful accomplishments, and of every branch of polite education, it has been long admitted, that a gentleman and lady never shew themselves to more advantage, than in acquitting themselves well in the honours of their table; that is to say, in serving their guests and treating their friends agreeable to their rank and situation in life.

Next to giving them a good dinner, is treating them with hospitality and attention, and this attention is what young people have to learn. Experience will teach them, in time, but till they learn, they will always appear ungraceful and awkward.

In all public companies precedence is attended to, and particularly at table. Women have here always taken place of men, and both men and women have sat above each other, according to the rank they bear in life. Where a company is equal in point of rank, married ladies take place of single ones, and older ones of younger ones.

When dinner is announced, the mistress of the house requests the lady first in rank, in company, to shew the way to the rest, and walk first into the room where the table is served; she then asks the second in precedence to follow, and after all the ladies are passed, she brings up the rear herself. The master of the house does the same with the gentlemen. Among persons of real distinction, this marshalling of the company is unnecessary, every woman and every man present knows his rank and precedence, and takes the lead, without any direction from the mistress or the master.

When they enter the dining-room, each takes his place in the same order; the mistress of the table sits at the upper-end, those of superior rank next her, right and left, those next in rank following, then the gentlemen, and the master at the lower-end; and nothing is considered as a greater mark of ill-breeding, than for a person to interrupt this order, or seat himself higher than he ought. Custom, however, has lately introduced a new mode of seating. A gentleman and a lady sitting alternately round the table, and this, for the better convenience of a lady's being attended to, and served by the gentleman next her. But notwithstanding this promiscuous seating, the ladies, whether above or below, are to be served in order, according to their rank or age, and after them the gentlemen, in the same manner.

The mistress of the house always sits at the upper-end of her table, provided any ladies are present, and her husband at the lower-end; but, if the company consists of gentlemen only, the mistress seldom appears, in which case, the master takes the upper-seat. *Note.* At whatever part of the table the mistress of the house sits, that will ever be considered as the first place.

As eating a great deal is deemed indelicate in a lady; (for her character should be rather divine than sensual,) it will be ill-manners to help her to a large slice of meat at once, or fill her plate too full. When you have served her with meat, she should be asked what kind of vegetables she likes, and the gentleman sitting next the dish that holds those vegetables, should be requested to help her.

Where there are several dishes at table, the mistress of the house carves that which is before her, and desires her husband, or the person at the bottom of the table, to carve the joint or bird, before *him*. Soup is generally the first thing served, and should be stirred from the bottom; fish, if there is any, the next.

5

The master or mistress of the table should continue eating, whilst any of the company are so employed, and to enable them to do this, they should help themselves accordingly.

Where there are not two courses, but one course and a remove, that is, a dish to be brought up, when one is taken away; the mistress or person who presides, should acquaint her company with what is to come; or if the whole is put on the table at once, should tell her friends, that "they see their dinner"; but, they should be told, what wine or other liquors is on the side-board. Sometimes a cold joint of meat, or a sallad, is placed on the side-board. In this case, it should be announced to the company.

If any of the company seem backward in asking for wine, it is the part of the master to ask or invite them to drink, or he will be thought to grudge his liquor; as it is the part of the mistress or master to ask those friends who seem to have dined, whether they would please to have more. As it is unseemly in ladies to call for wine, the gentlemen present should ask them in turn, whether it is agreeable to drink a glass of wine. ("Mrs.———, will you do me the honour to drink a glass of wine with me?") and what kind of the wine present they prefer, and call for two glasses of such wine, accordingly. Each then waits till the other is served, when they bow to each other and drink.

Habit having made a pint of wine after dinner almost necessary to a man who eats freely, which is not the case with women, and as their sitting and drinking with the men, would be unseemly; it is customary, after the cloth and desert are removed and two or three glasses of wine are gone round, for the ladies to retire and leave the men to themselves, and for this, 'tis the part of the mistress of the house to make the motion for retiring, by privately consulting the ladies present, whether they please to withdraw. The ladies thus rising, the men should rise of course, and the gentleman next the door should open it, to let them pass.

THE
ART OF CARVING

The author of this work, from a con-
viction that the knowledge it communi-
cates, is one of the accomplishments of
a gentleman, and that the *Art of Carving*
is little known, but to those who have
long been accustomed to it, persuades
himself, he cannot make the rising generation a more useful or acceptable present, than to lay before them a book,
that will teach them to acquit themselves
well, in the discharge of this part of the
honours of the table. (See the motto in
the title-page.) We are always in pain
for a man, who, instead of cutting up a
fowl genteely, is hacking for half an hour

9

across a bone, greasing himself, and bespattering the company with the sauce:
but where the master or mistress of a
table dissects a bird with ease and grace,
or serves her guest with such parts as
are best flavoured and most esteemed,
they are not only well thought of, but
admired. The principal things that are
brought then to table are here delineated,
and the customary method of carving
them pointed out, in a manner that, with
a little attention, will be readily under-
stood, and the knowledge of carving,
with a little practice, easily acquired.

Young folks unaccustomed to serving at table, will, with the help of the
cuts, and the instructions accompanying
them, soon be able to carve well, if at
the same time they will, as occasion
offers, take notice, how a good carver

proceeds, when a joint or fowl is before him.

I have also taken the liberty of pointing out in the course of these instructions, what parts of viands served up are most esteemed, that persons carving, may be enabled to shew a proper attention to their best guests and friends, and may help them to their liking.

There are some graceful methods of carving, that should also be attended to, such as not to rise from our seat, if we can help it, but to have a seat high enough to give us a command of the table; not to help any one to too much at a time; not to give the nice parts all to one person; but, to distribute them, if possible, among the whole, or the best to those of superior rank, in preference to those of inferior, and not to cut the slices too

11

thick or too thin, and to help them to gravy, removing the cold fat that swims on it, in cold weather; but it is generally best to ask our friends what part they like best.

We will then begin with those joints, &c. that are simple and easy to be carved, and afterwards proceed to such as are more complicate and difficult.

LEG OF MUTTON

This cut represents a leg or *Jigot* of boiled mutton, it should be served up in the dish as it here lies, lying upon it's back; and when roasted, the under-side, as here represented by the letter *d*, should lie uppermost in the dish, as in a ham, (which see, p. 33) and in this case, as it will be necessary occasionally to turn it so, as to get readily at the under side, and cut it in the direction *a*, *b*, the shank, which is here broken and bent, for the conveniency of putting into a less pot

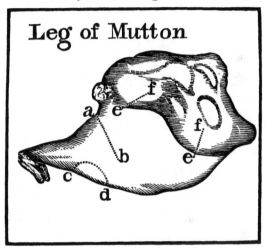

Leg of Mutton

or vessel to boil it, is not broken or bent in a roasted joint, of course, should be wound round, (after it is taken off the spit,) with half a sheet of writing paper, and so sent up to table, that the person carving it may take hold of it, without greasing his hands. Accordingly, when he wishes to cut it on the under-side, it being too heavy a joint to be easily turned with a fork, the carver is to take hold of the shank with his left hand, and he will thus be able to turn it readily, so as to cut it where he pleases with his right.

A leg of weather-mutton, which is by far the best flavoured, may be readily known when bought, by the kernel, or little round lump of fat, just above the letters *a, e*.

When a leg of mutton is first cut, the person carving should turn the joint to-wards him as it here lies, the shank to the left hand; then holding it steady with his fork, he should cut it deep on the fleshy part, in the hollow of the thigh, quite to the bone, in the direction *a, b*.

14

Thus will he cut right through the kernel of fat, called the *Pope's-eye*, which many are fond of. The most juicy parts of the leg, are in the thick part of it, from the line *a*, *b*, upwards, towards *e*, but many prefer the dryer part, which is about the shank or knuckle; this part is by far the coarser, but as I said, some prefer it and call it the venison part, tho' it is less like venison than any other part of the joint. The fat of this joint lies chiefly on the ridge *e*, *e*, and is to be cut in the direction *e*, *f*.

As many are fond of having a bone, and have an idea, that the nearer the bone, the sweeter the flesh; in a leg of mutton, there is but one bone readily to be got at, and that a small one; this is the *Cramp-bone*, by some called the *Gentleman's-bone*, and is to be cut out,

15

by taking hold of the shank-bone with the left hand, and with a knife, cutting down to the thigh-bone at the point d, then passing the knife under the cramp-bone, in the direction d, c, it may easily be cut out.

SHOULDER OF MUTTON
No. 1

Figure 1 represents a shoulder of mutton, which is sometimes salted and boiled by fanciful people; but customarily served up roasted, and is laid in the dish, with the back or upper-side uppermost, as here.

When not over-roasted, it is a joint very full of gravy, much more so than a leg, and as such, by many preferred, and particularly as having many very good, delicate, and savory parts in it.

16

The shank-bone should be wound round with writing-paper as pointed out in the leg, that the person carving may take hold of it, to turn it as he wishes.

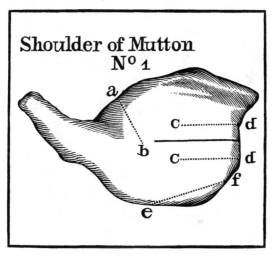

Shoulder of Mutton
Nº 1

Now, when it is first cut, it should be in the hollow part of it, in the direction *a, b,* and the knife should be passed deep to the bone. The gravy then runs fast into the dish, and the part cut opens wide

enough, to take many slices from it
readily.

The best fat, that which is full of kernels and best flavoured, lies on the outer-
edge, and is to be cut out in thin slices
in the direction *e*, *f*. If many are at table,
and the hollow part cut in the line *a*, *b*,
is all eaten, some very good and delicate
slices may be cut out, on each side the
ridge of the blade-bone, in the directions
c, *d*. The line between these two dotted
lines is that, in the direction of which the
edge or ridge of the blade-bone lies, and
cannot be cut across.

On the under-side of the shoulder, as
represented below, in figure 2 there are
two parts, very full of gravy, and such
as many persons prefer to those of the
upper-side. One is a deep cut, in the
direction *g*, *h*, accompanied with fat, and

18

the other all lean, in a line from *i*, to *k*. The parts about the shank are coarse and dry, as about the knuckle in the leg; but

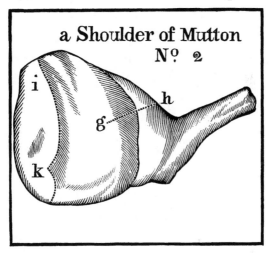

yet some prefer this dry part, as being less rich or luscious, and of course, less apt to cloy.

A shoulder of mutton over-roasted is spoilt.

A LEG OF PORK

Whether boiled or roasted, is sent up to table as a leg of mutton roasted, and cut up in the same manner; of course, I shall refer you to what I have said upon that joint, only that the close, firm flesh about the knuckle, is by many reckoned the best, which is not the case in a leg of mutton.

A shoulder of Pork is never cut or sent to table as such, but the shank-bone, with some little meat annexed, is often served up boiled, and called a Spring, and is very good eating.

EDGE BONE OF BEEF

As this work is not a critical investigation of words, but relates merely to the art of carving, I shall not give my reasons

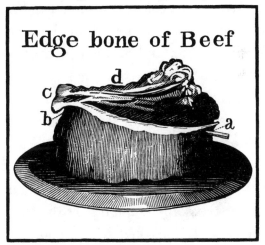

Edge bone of Beef

for calling it an *Edge-bone*, in preference to *Ridge-bone*, *Each-bone*, or *Ach-bone*, but have given it that, by which it is generally known. The above is a representation of it, and is a favourite joint at table.

In carving it, as the outside suffers in it's flavour, from the water in which it is boiled, the dish should be turned towards the carver, as it is here represented; and a thick slice should be first cut off, the whole length of the joint, beginning at *a*, and cutting it all the way even and through the whole surface, from *a* to *b*.

The soft fat that resembles marrow, lies on the back, below the letter *d*, and the firm fat is to be cut in thin horizontal slices at the point *c*; but, as some persons prefer the soft fat, and others the firm, each should be asked what he likes.

The upper-part as here shewn, is certainly the handsomest, fullest of gravy, most tender, and is encircled with fat; but, there are still some, who prefer a slice on the under-side, which is quite lean.

But, as it is a heavy joint and very trouble-some to turn, that person cannot have much good manners, who requests it.

The skewer that keeps the meat together when boiling, is here shewn at *a*. It should be drawn out, before the dish is served up to table; or, if it is necessary to leave a skewer in, that skewer should be a silver one.

A SADDLE OF MUTTON

This is by some called a chine of mutton, the saddle being the two necks, but as the two necks are now seldom sent to table together, they call the two loins a saddle.

A saddle of mutton is a genteel and handsome dish, it consists of the two loins together, the back-bone running down the middle, to the tail. Of course, when it is to be carved, you must cut a long slice in either of the fleshy parts, on the side of the back-bone, in the direction a, b.

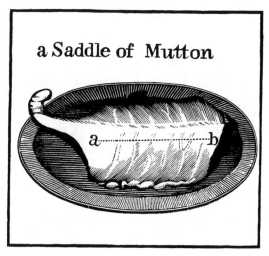

a Saddle of Mutton

There is seldom any great length of the tail left on, but if it is sent up with the tail, many are fond of it, and it may readily be divided into several pieces, by cutting between the joints of the tail, which are about the distance of one inch apart.

24

A BREAST OF VEAL
ROASTED

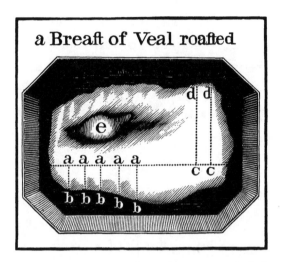

a Breaſt of Veal roaſted

This is the best end of a breast of veal, with the sweet-bread lying on it, and when carved, should be first cut across quite through, in the line *a, c*, dividing the gristles from the rib-bones: this done, to those who like fat and gristle,

the thick or gristly part should be cut
into pieces as wanted, in the lines a, b.
When a breast of veal is cut into pieces
and stewed, these gristles are very tender and eatable. To such persons as
prefer a bone, a rib should be cut or
separated from the rest in the lines d, c,
and with a part of the breast, a slice of
the sweet-bread e, cut across the middle.

A KNUCKLE OF VEAL

A knuckle of veal is always boiled,
and is admired for the fat, sinewy tendons about the knuckle, which if boiled
tender, are much esteemed. A lean
knuckle is not worth the dressing.

You cannot cut a handsome slice, but
in the direction a, b. The most delicate
fat lies about the part d, and if cut in the

line *d*, *c*, you will divide two bones, between which, lies plenty of fine marrowy
fat.

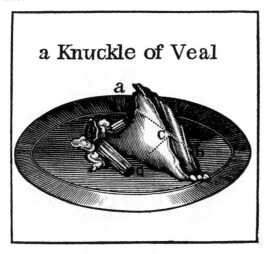

a Knuckle of Veal

The several bones about the knuckle,
may be readily separated at the joints,
and as they are covered with tendons,
a bone may be given to those who like it.

A spare-rib of pork is carved, by cutting out a slice from the fleshy part, in the line *a, b.* This joint will afford many

a Spare-rib of Pork

good cuts in this direction, with as much fat; as people like to eat of such strong meat. When the fleshy part is cut away, a bone may be easily separated from the next to it, in the line *d, b, c,* disjointing it at *c.*

Few pork-eaters are fond of gravy, it being too strong, on this account, it is eaten with apple-sauce.

HALF A CALF'S HEAD BOILED

There are many delicate bits about a calf's head, and when young, perfectly white, fat, and well-dressed, half a head is a genteel dish.

When first cut, it should be quite along the cheek-bone, in the fleshy part, in the direction c, b, where many handsome slices may be cut. In the fleshy part, at the end of the jaw-bone, lies part of the throat sweet-bread, which may be cut into, in the line c, d, and which is esteemed the best part in the head. Many like the eye, which is to be cut from it's socket a, by forcing the point of a carving knife

29

down to the bottom on one edge, of the socket, and cutting quite round, keeping the point of the knife slanting towards the middle, so as to separate the meat

Half a Calf's Head boild.

from the bone. This piece is seldom divided, but if you wish to oblige two persons with it, it may be cut into two parts. The palate is also reckoned by some a delicate morsel; this is found on the under-side of the roof of the mouth, it is a crinkled, white thick skin, and may be easily separated from the bone by the knife, by lifting the head up with your left hand.

There is also some good meat to be met with on the under-side, covering the under-jaw, and some nice, gristly fat to be pared off about the ear, g.

There are scarce any bones here to be separated; but one may be cut off, at the neck, in the line f, e, but this is a coarse part.

There is a tooth in the upper-jaw, the last tooth behind, which having several cells, and being full of jelly, is called the sweet-tooth. It's delicacy is more in the name than any thing else. It is a double tooth, lies firm in a socket, at the further end, but if the calf was a young one, may

31

readily be taken out with the point of a knife.

In serving your guest with a slice of head, you should enquire whether he would have any of the tongue or brains, which are generally served up in a separate dish, in which case, a slice from the thick part of the tongue near the root is best. Sometimes the brains are made up into small cakes, fried, and put round the head to ornament it; when so, give one of these cakes.

A H A M

A ham is cut two ways, across in the line b, c, or, with the point of the carving knife, in the circular line in the middle, taking out a small piece as at a, and cutting thin slices in a circular direction, thus enlarging it by degrees. This last method of cutting it, is to preserve the gravy and keep it moist, which is thus prevented from running out.

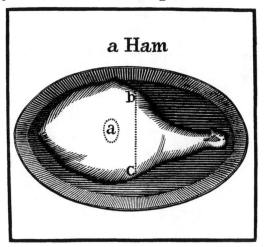

A HAUNCH OF VENISON

In carving a haunch of venison, first cut it across down to the bone, in the line *d*, *c*, *a*, then turn the dish with the

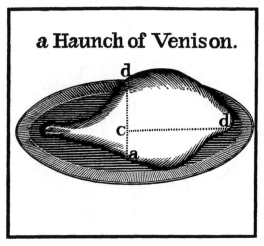

a Haunch of Venison.

end *d*, towards you, put in the point of the knife at *c*, and cut it down as deep as you can in the direction *c*, *d*; thus cut, you may take out as many slices as you please, on the right or left. As the fat lies deeper on the left, between d and a, to those who are fond of fat, as most venison-eaters are, the best flavoured and fattest slices will be found on the left of the line c, d, supposing the end d, turned towards you. Slices of venison should not be cut thick, nor too thin, and plenty of gravy should be given with them; but, as there is a particular sauce made for this meat, with red wine and currant jelly; your guest should be asked, if he pleases to have any.

As the fat of venison is very apt to cool and get hard and disagreeable to the palate, it should always be served up on a water-dish, and if your company is large, and the joint is a long time on the table, a lamp should be sent for, and a few slices, fat and lean with some of the gravy, is presently heated over it, either in a silver or a pewter plate. This is always done at table, and the sight of the lamp, never fails to give pleasure to your company.

AN OX TONGUE

A tongue is to be cut across, in the line *a b*, and a slice taken from thence. The most tender and juicy slices will be

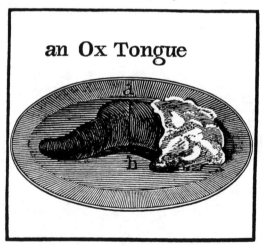

an Ox Tongue

about the middle, or between the line
a b, and the root. Towards the tip, the
meat is closer and dryer. For the fat,
and a kernel with that fat, cut off a slice
of the root, on the right of the letter *b*,
at the bottom next the dish. A tongue
is generally eaten with white meat, veal,
chicken, or turkey, and to those whom
you serve with the latter, you should
give a slice of the former.

SIRLOIN OF BEEF

Whether the whole sirloin or part of
it only be sent to table, is immaterial,
with respect to carving it. The figure
here represents part of the joint only,
the whole being too large for families
in general. It is drawn as standing up
in the dish, in order to shew the inside

37

or under-part; but when sent to table it is always laid down, so as that the part described by the letter *c*, lies close on

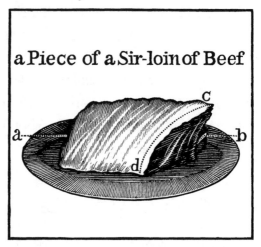

a Piece of a Sir-loin of Beef

the dish. The part *c d*, then lies uppermost, and the line *a b*, underneath.

The meat on the upper-side of the ribs is firmer, and of a closer texture, than the fleshy part underneath, which is by far the most tender; of course, some prefer one part, and some the other.

To those who like the upper-side and would rather not have the first cut or outside slice, that outside slice should be first cut off, quite down to the bone, in the direction cd. Plenty of soft, marrowy fat will be found underneath the ribs. If a person wishes to have a slice underneath, the joint must be turned up, by taking hold of the end of the ribs with the left hand, and raising it, till it is in the position as here represented. One slice or more may now be cut in the direction of the line ab, passing the knife down to the bone. The slices, whether on the upper or under side, should be cut thin, but not too much so.

A BRISKET OF BEEF

This is a part always boiled, and is to be cut in the direction *a b*, quite down to the bone, but never help any one to

a Brisket of Beef

the outside slice, which should be taken off pretty thick. The fat cut with this slice is a firm gristly fat, but a softer fat will be found underneath, for those who prefer it.

A BUTTOCK OF BEEF

Is always boiled, and requires no print to point out how it should be carved. A thick slice should be cut off all round the buttock, that your friends may be helped to the juicy and prime part of it. Thus cut into, thin slices may be cut from the top; but, as it is a dish that is frequently brought to table cold, a second day, it should always be cut handsome and even. To those to whom a slice all round would be too much, a third of the round may be given, with a thin slice of fat. On one side there is a part whiter than ordinary, by some called the white muscle. In *Wiltshire* and the neighbouring counties, a bullock is generally divided, and this white part sold separate as a delicacy, but it is by no means so, the meat being close and dry, whereas

41

the darker coloured parts, though apparently of a coarser grain, are of a looser texture, more tender, fuller of gravy, and better flavoured; and, men of distinguishing palates, ever prefer them.

A FILLET OF VEAL

Which is the thigh part, similar to a buttock of beef, is brought to table always in the same form, but roasted. The outside slice of the fillet, is by many thought a delicacy, as being most savoury; but, it does not follow, that every one likes it; each person should therefore be asked, what part they prefer. If not the outside, cut off a thin slice, and the second cut will be white meat, but cut it even and close to the bone. A fillet of veal is generally stuffed under the skirt or flap with a savoury pudding, called forced-meat. This is to be cut deep into, in a line with the surface of the fillet, and a thin slice taken out; this, with a little fat cut from the skirt, should be given to each person present.

A FORE QUARTER OF LAMB ROASTED

Before any one is helped to part of this joint, the shoulder should be separated from the breast, or what is by some called the coast; by passing the knife under, in the direction *c*, *g*, *d*, *e*. The shoulder being thus removed, a lemon or orange should be squeezed upon the part, and then sprinkled with salt where the shoulder joined it, and the shoulder should be laid on it again. The gristly

part should next be separated from the
ribs, in the line *f, d*. It is now in readi-
ness to be divided among the company.
The ribs are generally most esteemed,

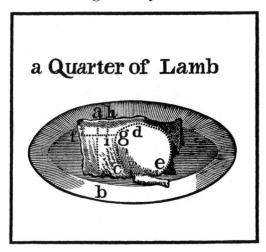

a **Quarter of Lamb**

and one or two may be separated from
the rest, in the line *a b*; or, to those who
prefer the gristly part, a piece or two,
or more, may be cut off in the lines, *b*,
i, &c. Though all parts of young lamb

are nice, the shoulder of a fore-quarter is the least thought of; it is not so rich.

If the fore-quarter is that of grass lamb and large, the shoulder should be put into another dish, when taken off, and it is carved, as a shoulder of mutton, which see.

A ROASTED PIG

A roasted pig is seldom sent to table whole, the head is cut off by the cook, and the body split down the back, and served up as here represented; and the dish garnished, with the chaps and ears.

Before any one is helped, the shoulder should be separated from the carcase, by passing the knife under it, in the circular direction; and the leg separated in the same manner, in the dotted line c, d, e.

The most delicate part of the whole pig, is the triangular piece of the neck, which may be cut off in the line f,g. The next best parts are the ribs, which may be

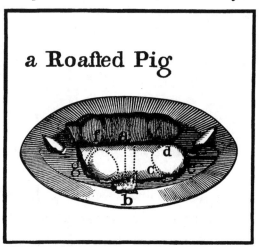

a Roasted Pig

divided in the line $a\ b$, &c. Indeed, the bones of a pig of three weeks old, are little else than gristle, and may easily be cut through; next to these, are pieces cut from the leg and shoulder. Some are fond of an ear, and others of a chap, and those persons may readily be gratified.

A H A R E

This is a hare as trussed and sent up to table. A skewer is run through two shoulders, (or wings as some call them,) the point of which is shewn at *d*, another is passed through the mouth at *a*, into the body, to keep the head in it's place; and two others, through the roots of the ears, in the direction *b f*, to keep the ears erect. These skewers are seldom removed till the hare is cut up.

Now, there are two ways of cutting it up. The genteelest, best and readiest way, is as above described, to put in the point of the knife at *g*, and cut it through all the way down to the rump, on one side the back-bone, in the line *g h*. This done, cut it similarly on the other side, at an equal distance from the back-bone. The body is thus divided into three. You have now an opportunity of cutting the

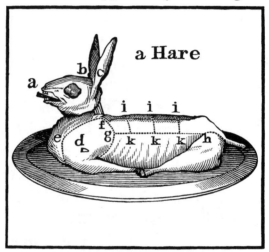

back through the spine or back-bone, into several small pieces, more or less in the lines *i k*, the back being by far the tenderest part, fullest of gravy, and the greatest delicate. With a part of the back should be given a spoonful of pudding, with which the belly is stuffed, below the letters k, and which is now easily to be got at. Having thus separated the legs from the back-bone, they are easily cut from the belly. The legs are the parts next in estimation, but their meat is closer, firmer and less juicy. The shoulders or wings are to be cut off in the circular dotted line $e\ f\ g$. The shoulders are generally bloody ; but many like the blood, and of course, prefer the shoulder to the leg. In a large hare, a whole leg is too much to be given to any one person at one time, it should therefore be divided, and the best part of the leg, is the fleshy part of the thigh at b, which should be cut off.

Some like the head, brains and bloody part of the neck, before then you begin to dissect the head, cut off the ears at the roots, which if roasted crisp, many are fond of, and may be asked if they please to have one.

Now the head should be divided; for this purpose it should be taken on a clean plate, so as to be under your hand, and turning the nose to you, hold it steady with your fork, that it does not flie from under the knife; you are then to put the point of the knife into the skull between the ears, and by forcing it down, as soon as it has made it's way, you may easily divide the head into two, by cutting with some degree of strength quite down through to the nose. Half the head may be given to any person that likes it.

But this mode of cutting up a hare can only be done with ease, when the animal is young. If it be an old hare, the best method is, to put your knife pretty close to the back-bone, and cut off one leg, but as the hip-bone will be in your way, the back of the hare must be turned towards you, and you must endeavour to hit the joint between the hip and the thigh-bone. When you have separated one, cut off the other, then cut out a long narrow slice or two on each side the back-bone, in the direction g h; this done, divide the back-bone into two, three, or more parts, passing your knife between the several joints of the back, which may readily be effected with a little attention and patience.

A RABBIT

Is trussed like a hare, and cut up in the same way, only as being much smaller, after the legs are separated

from the body, the back is divided into
two or three parts, without dividing it
from the belly, but cutting it in the line
g h, as in the hare; and, instead of dividing the head in two, a whole head is
given to a person who likes it, the ears
being removed, before the rabbit is
served up.

A GOOSE

Like a turkey, is seldom quite dis-
sected, unless the company is large; but
when it is, the following is the method.
Turn the neck towards you, and cut two
or three long slices, on each side the
breast, in the lines *a b*, quite to the bone.
Cut these slices from the bone, which
done, proceed to take off the leg, by
turning the goose upon one side, putting
the fork through the small end of the leg-

bone, pressing it close to the body, which
when the knife is entered at *d* raises the
joint from the body. The knife is then
to be passed under the leg in the direc-

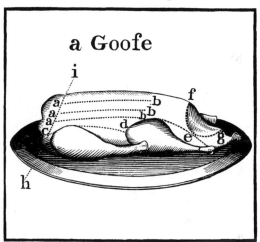

tion *d e*. If the leg hangs to the carcase
at the joint *e*, turn it back with the fork,
and it will readily separate, if the goose
is young: in an old goose it will require
some strength to separate it. When the

leg is off, proceed to take off the wing, by passing the fork through the small end of the pinion, pressing it close to the body and entering the knife at the notch *c* and passing it under the wing in the direction *c d*. It is a nice thing to hit this notch *c*, as it is not so visible in the bird as in the figure. If the knife is put into the notch above it, you cut upon the neck bone and not on the wing joint.

A little practice will soon teach the difference, and if the goose is young, the trouble is not great, but very much otherwise, if the bird is an old one.

When the leg and wing on one side are taken off, take them off on the other side; cut off the apron in the line *f e g*, and then take off the merry-thought in the line *i h*. The neck-bones are next to be separated as in a fowl, and all the other parts divided as there directed, to which I refer you.

The best parts of a goose are in the following order; the breast slices; the fleshy part of the wing, which may be divided from the pinion; the thigh-bone, which may be easily divided in the joint from the leg-bone, or drum-stick, as it is called, the pinion, and next the side-bones. To those who like sage and onion, draw it out with a spoon from the body, at the place where the apron is taken from, and mix it with the gravy, which should first be poured from the boat into the body of the goose, before any one is helped. The rump is a nice bit to those who like it. It is often peppered and salted, and sent down to be boiled, and is then called a Devil, as I have mentioned in speaking of a turkey.

Even the carcase of a goose, by some, is preferred to other parts, as being more juicy and more savory.

A GREEN GOOSE

Is cut up the same way, but the most delicate part is the breast and the gristle, at the lower part of it.

A PHEASANT

The pheasant as here represented, is skewered and trussed for the spit, with the head tucked under one of the wings, but when sent to table, the skewers are withdrawn.

In carving this bird, the fork should be fixed in the breast, in the two dots there marked. You have then the command of the fowl, and can turn it as you please; slice down the breast in the lines

56

a,*b*, and then proceed to take off the leg on one side, in the direction *d*, *e*, or in the circular dotted line *b d*, as seen in the figure of the fowl, page 62. This

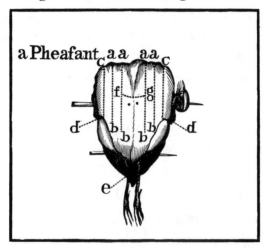

done, cut off the wing on the same side, in the line *c d*, in the figure above, and *a b b*, in the figure of the fowl, page 62, which is represented lying on one side, with it's back towards us. Having separated the leg and wing on one side, do the same on the other, and then cut off, or separate from the breast-bone, on each side of the breast, the parts you before sliced or cut down. In taking off the wing, be attentive, and cut it in the notch a, as seen in the print of the fowl; for, if you cut too near the neck, as at g, you will find the neck-bone interfere. The wing is to be separated from the neck-bone. Next cut off the merry-thought in the line fg, by passing the knife under it towards the neck. The remaining parts are to be cut up, as is described in the fowl, which see. Some persons like the head, for the sake of the brains. A pheasant is seldom all cut up, but the several parts separated, as they are found to be wanted.

The best parts of a pheasant, are the

white parts, first the breast, next the wings, and next the merry-thought; but, if your company is large, in order to distribute the parts equally between them, give part of a leg, with a slice of the breast, or a side's-bone with the merry-thought, or divide the wing in two, cutting off part of the white, fleshy part from the pinion.

A PARTRIDGE

The partridge, like the pheasant, is here trussed for the spit; when served up, the skewers are withdrawn. It is cut up like a fowl, (which see,) the wings taken off in the lines $a, b,$ and the merry-thought in the line $c, d.$ Of a partridge, the prime parts are the white ones, *viz.* the wings, breast and merry-thought. The wing is thought the best, the tip

being reckoned the most delicate morsel of the whole. If your company is
large, and you have but a brace of birds,
rather than give offence, in distributing

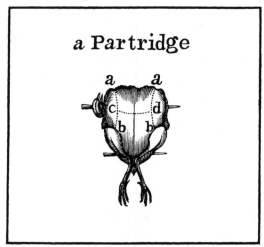

a Partridge

the several parts amongst them, the
most politic method is to cut up the
brace, agreeable to the directions given
for cutting up a fowl; and sending a
plate with the several parts round to

your company, according to their rank, or the respect you bear them. Their modesty then will lead them not to take the best parts, and he that is last served, will stand a chance to get the nicest bit; for, a person will perhaps take a leg himself, who would be offended, if you sent him one.

A FOWL

The fowl is here represented as lying on it's side, with one of the legs, wings and neck-bone, taken off. It is cut up the same way, whether it be roasted or boiled. A roasted fowl is sent to table trussed like the pheasant, (which see,) except, that instead of the head being tucked under one of the wings, it is, in a fowl, cut off before it is dressed. A boiled fowl is represented below, the leg-bones of which are bent inwards, and tucked in, within the belly; but the skewers are withdrawn prior to it's being

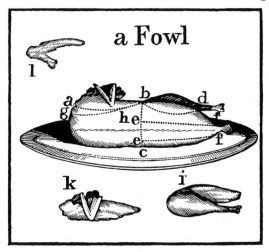

sent to table. In order to cut up a fowl, it is best to take it on your plate.

Having shewn how to take off the legs, wings and merry-thought, when speaking of the pheasant; it remains only to shew, how the other parts are divided, *k* is the wing cut off, *i* the leg. When the leg, wing and merry-thought are removed, the next thing is, to cut off the neck-bones described at *l*. This is done by putting in the knife at *g*, and passing it under the long broad part of the bone in the line *g b*, then lifting it up and breaking off the end of the shorter part of the bone, which cleaves to the breast-bone. All the parts being thus separated from the carcase, divide the breast from the back, by cutting through the tender ribs on each side, from the neck quite down to the vent or tail. Then lay the back upwards on your plate, fix your fork under the rump, and laying the edge of your knife in the line *b, e, c*, and pressing it down, lift up the tail or lower part of the back, and it will readily divide with the help of your knife, in the line *b*, *e*, *c*. This done, lay the croup or lower part of the back upwards in your plate, with the rump from you, and with your knife, cut off the side-bones, by

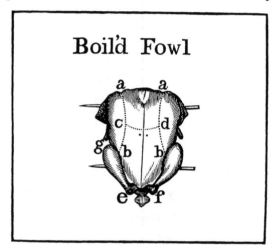

forcing the knife through the rump-bone, in the lines *e*, *f*, *e*, *f*, and the whole fowl is completely carved.

Of a fowl, the prime parts are the wings, breast and merry-thought, and next to these, the neck-bones and side-bones; the legs are rather coarse; of a boiled fowl, the legs are rather more tender, but of a chicken, every part is juicy and good, and next the breast, the legs are certainly the fullest of gravy, and the sweetest; and, as the thigh-bones are very tender and easily broken with the teeth, the gristles and marrow render them a delicate. Of the leg of a fowl, the thigh is abundantly the best, and when given to any one of your company, it should be separated from the drum-stick, at the joint i; (see the cut p. 62;) which is easily done, if the knife is introduced underneath in the hollow, and the thigh-bone turned back from the leg-bone.

A TURKEY

Roasted or boiled, is trussed and sent up to table like a fowl, and cut up in every respect like a pheasant. The best parts are the white ones, the breast, wings and neck-bones. Merry-thought it has none; the neck is taken away, and the hollow part under the breast stuffed with force-meat, which is to be cut in thin slices, in the direction from the rump to the neck, and a slice given with each piece of turkey. It is customary not to cut up more than the breast of this bird, and if any more is wanted, to take off one of the wings.

Some epicures are very fond of the gizzard and rump, peppered well and salted and broiled, which they call a *Devil*. When this is to be done, it is

generally cut a little way in the sub-
stance, in several parts of it, with the
knife, peppered and salted a little, and
sent down to be broiled, and when
brought up, is divided into parts and
handed round to the company, as a
bonne bouche.

A PIDGEON

This is the representation of the back
and breast of a pidgeon. No. 1 the
back. No. 2 the breast. It is sometimes cut up as a chicken, but as the
croup or lower-part, with the thigh, is
most preferred, and as a pidgeon is a
small bird, and half a one not too much
to serve at once, it is seldom carved
now, otherwise than by fixing the fork
at the point *a*, entering the knife just
before it, and dividing the pidgeon into

two, cutting away in the lines *a b*, and
a c, No. 1; at the same time, bringing

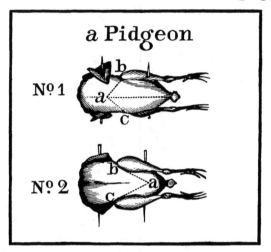

the knife out at the back, in the direction *a b*, and *a c*, No. 2.

A C O D'S H E A D

Fish, in general, requires very little
carving, the middle or thickest part of
a fish, is generally esteemed the best,

except in a carp, the most delicate part of which is the palate. This is seldom

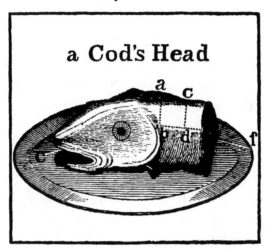

a Cod's Head

however taken out, but the whole head is given, to those who like it. The thin parts about the tail of a fish are generally least esteemed.

A cod's head and shoulders, if large, and in season, is a very genteel and handsome dish, if nicely boiled. When

69

cut, it should be done with a spoon or fish-trowel, the parts about the back-bone on the shoulders, are the most firm and best; take off a piece quite down to the bone, in the direction *a*, *b*, *d*, *c*, putting in the spoon at *a c*, and with each slice of fish give a piece of the sound, which lies underneath the back-bone and lines it, the meat of which is thin and a little darker coloured, than the body of the fish itself; this may be got, by passing a knife or spoon under-neath, in the direction *d f*.

There are a great many delicate parts about the head, some firm kernels, and a great deal of the jelly kind. The jelly parts lie about the jaw-bones, the firm parts within the head, which must be broken into with a spoon. Some like the palate and some the tongue, which

70

likewise may be got, by putting a spoon into the mouth, in the direction of the line *f*. The green jelly of the eye is never given to any one.

BOILED SALMON

Of boiled salmon, there is one part more fat and rich than the other. The belly part is the fattest of the two, and

aPiece of Boiled Salmon

it is customary to give to those who like both, a thin slice of each; the one cut out of the belly part in the direction dc, the other out of the back in the line ab. Those who are fond of salmon, generally like the skin, of course, the slices are to be cut out thin, skin and all.

There are but few directions necessary for cutting up and serving fish. In *Turbot*, the fish-knife or trowel is to be entered in the center or middle over the back-bone, and a piece of the fish, as much as will lie on the trowel, to be taken off on one side close to the bones. The thickest part of the fish is always most esteemed, but not too near the head or tail; and, when the meat on one side of the fish is removed close to the bones, the whole back-bone is to be raised with the knife and fork, and the under-side is then to be divided among the company. Turbot-eaters esteem the fins a delicate part.

Soals are generally sent to table two ways, some fried, others boiled; these are to be cut right through the middle, bone and all, and a piece of the fish, perhaps a third or fourth part, according to it's size, given to each. The same may be done with other fish, cutting them across, as may be seen in the cut of the mackrell, below *d e*, *c b*, page 74.

A MACKRELL

A mackrell is to be thus cut. Slit the fish all along the back with a knife in the line *a e b*, and take off one whole side, as far as the line *b c*, not too near the head, as the meat about the gills is generally black and ill-flavoured. The

73

roe of a male fish is soft like the brain
of a calf, the roe of the female fish is full
of small eggs, and hard. Some prefer
one and some another, and part of such

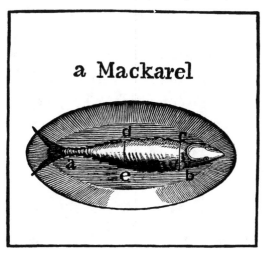

a Mackarel

roe as your friend likes should be given
to him.

The meat, about the tail of all fish,
is generally thin and least esteemed,
and few like the head of a fish, except

it be that of a Carp, the palate of which is esteemed the greatest delicacy of the whole.

Eels are cut into pieces through the bone, and the thickest part is reckoned the prime piece.

There is some art in dressing a *Lobster*, but as this is seldom sent up to table whole, I will only say, that the tail is reckoned the prime part, and next to this the claws.

There are many little directions that might be given to young people with respect to other articles brought to table; but, as observation will be their best director, in matters simple in themselves, I shall not swell this work in pointing them out. Where there is any difficulty in carving I have endeavoured to remove it, and trust, that the rules I have laid down will, with a little practice, make the reader a proficient in this art, which may be truly called a polite accomplishment.

TRUSLER

Printed in the United States
By Bookmasters